THE FUNDAMENTAL GUIDE TO SEXTANT

The Secret To Sea Voyage And The Men Who Mapped The World's Oceans

Sailor George

Table of Contents

CHAPTER ONE

Introduction to the Sextant

History and Invention: Overview of the Sextant's Invention and Early Development

The sextant, a crucial navigational instrument, revolutionized maritime exploration by allowing sailors to determine their precise location at sea. Its invention and development marked a significant leap forward in the history of navigation, directly impacting the Age of Exploration and beyond.

Early Navigation Challenges

Before the sextant, mariners relied on rudimentary tools such as the astrolabe, cross-staff, and quadrant. These instruments, while innovative for their time, had significant limitations in terms of accuracy and ease of use. Navigators could determine their latitude by measuring the angle between the horizon and a celestial body like the sun or a star, but these tools were often cumbersome and less reliable under various sea conditions.

The Problem of Longitude

The determination of longitude posed a particularly vexing problem for early navigators. Unlike latitude, which could be gauged by celestial bodies' position relative to the horizon, longitude required precise timekeeping in relation to a fixed meridian. Without an accurate way to measure time at sea, determining one's east-west position remained highly imprecise, often leading to perilous navigation errors.

Invention of the Sextant

The quest to solve these navigational challenges led to the development of the sextant in the mid-18th century. The sextant's invention is attributed to two individuals: John Hadley, an English mathematician, and Thomas Godfrey, an American inventor. Independently, both men developed versions of the reflecting quadrant around 1730, which later evolved into the modern sextant.

John Hadley's design involved a double-reflecting principle, using mirrors to bring two images together.

This principle allowed for the measurement of angles up to 120 degrees between celestial objects and the horizon with much greater accuracy than previous instruments. Thomas Godfrey's version was similar in concept, and both inventions signaled a major advancement in navigational tools.

Development and Refinement

Over the subsequent decades, the sextant underwent further refinements. Its arc was expanded to allow for wider angle measurements, and the inclusion of a vernier scale improved the precision of readings. The addition of a telescope enhanced the visibility of celestial objects, making it easier to take accurate measurements even under less-than-ideal conditions.

Basic Principles: Explanation of the Sextant's Function and Importance in Navigation

The sextant operates on a relatively simple yet ingenious principle, utilizing a system of mirrors to measure the angle between two visible objects.

This capability is essential for celestial navigation, enabling sailors to determine their position on the globe by observing the sun, stars, planets, or the moon.

Components of the Sextant

A sextant consists of several key components:

1. **Frame**: The backbone of the instrument, typically made from brass or aluminum, ensuring rigidity and durability.

2. **Arc**: A graduated scale marked in degrees, usually spanning 60 degrees but allowing measurements up to 120 degrees thanks to the reflection principle.

3. **Index Arm**: A movable arm pivoting at the center of the arc, carrying an index mirror and vernier scale.

4. **Index Mirror**: Mounted on the index arm, this mirror reflects the image of the celestial body.

5. **Horizon Mirror**: Half-silvered, allowing the observer to see the horizon directly and the reflected image of the celestial body simultaneously.

6. **Telescope**: Attached to the frame, it aids in sighting the celestial body and the horizon.

7. **Screw and Clamp**: Used to lock the index arm in place once the desired angle is measured.

8. **Shade Glasses**: Filters to protect the observer's eyes from the sun's glare.

How It Works

To use a sextant, the navigator follows these steps:

1. **Sight the Horizon**: The observer looks through the telescope, aligning it with the horizon visible through the half-silvered horizon mirror.

2. **Align the Celestial Body**: The index arm is moved until the celestial body (sun, star, etc.) is visible through the index mirror and appears to touch the horizon in the telescope's view.

3. **Lock the Angle**: The index arm is clamped in place, and the precise angle between the horizon and the celestial body is read from the vernier scale on the arc.

4. **Calculate Position**: This angle, along with the time of the observation, is used to calculate the observer's latitude and longitude using astronomical tables or navigational charts.

Importance in Navigation

The sextant's ability to provide accurate measurements of celestial angles made it an indispensable tool for mariners. It allowed for:

- **Determination of Latitude**: By measuring the sun's angle at noon (its highest point in the sky) or the altitude of a known star, sailors could determine their latitude with high precision.

- **Calculation of Longitude**: Combined with an accurate timekeeping device (chronometer), the sextant enabled the calculation of longitude through methods like lunar distance, transforming oceanic navigation.

- **Reliability at Sea**: Unlike earlier instruments, the sextant's double-reflecting principle minimized errors caused by the ship's movement, making it reliable even in rough seas.

Impact on Exploration: How the Sextant Revolutionized Sea Travel and Exploration

The sextant's introduction had a profound impact on maritime navigation and exploration, facilitating safer and more accurate sea voyages. Its influence extended from the Age of Exploration to the scientific expeditions of the 19th century and beyond.

Enhanced Safety and Accuracy

Before the sextant, sailors often faced considerable risks due to the inaccuracy of navigational tools. Misjudging one's position could lead to shipwrecks, loss of cargo, and lives. The sextant significantly reduced these risks by providing precise measurements of celestial angles, allowing navigators to plot their courses with greater accuracy. This improvement in navigational precision translated into safer sea voyages, reduced travel time, and lower costs for maritime expeditions.

Expansion of Trade Routes

With the advent of the sextant, new trade routes could be established and existing ones navigated more efficiently. The ability to determine longitude accurately meant that ships could venture further into open seas with confidence, avoiding the perilous coastlines that had previously guided much of maritime travel. This capability opened up new markets and facilitated global trade, contributing to economic growth and the exchange of goods, cultures, and ideas across continents.

Exploration and Scientific Discovery

The sextant played a crucial role in the great voyages of exploration during the 18th and 19th centuries. Notable explorers like Captain James Cook relied heavily on the sextant to chart previously uncharted territories. Cook's voyages to the Pacific Ocean, New Zealand, and Australia were made possible by the sextant's precise navigational capabilities, leading to the detailed mapping of these regions.

Scientific expeditions also benefited from the sextant. Naturalists like Charles Darwin used precise navigational data to document and study the geographic distribution of species, contributing to the development of evolutionary theory. The sextant's accuracy enabled the collection of reliable data on the positions of islands, coastlines, and other geographical features, enriching the scientific knowledge of the time.

The Sextant in Naval Warfare

Naval powers quickly recognized the strategic advantages provided by the sextant. Accurate navigation was critical for naval operations, allowing fleets to maneuver with precision, coordinate movements, and engage in combat effectively. The sextant thus became an essential tool for naval officers, contributing to the success of maritime military campaigns.

Legacy and Continued Relevance

Even with the advent of electronic navigation systems like GPS, the sextant remains a symbol of traditional seafaring skills and ingenuity. Many modern sailors and navigators continue to learn and practice celestial navigation as a backup method, recognizing the sextant's reliability in the event of electronic failure. Its legacy endures in maritime education, preserving the techniques and knowledge that once revolutionized sea travel.

The sextant's invention and development marked a transformative period in the history of navigation, overcoming the limitations of earlier tools and enabling precise sea travel. By understanding its basic principles and appreciating its impact on exploration, one can grasp the profound significance of the sextant in maritime history. This chapter has provided an overview of the sextant's invention, explained its fundamental mechanics, and highlighted its revolutionary role in navigation and exploration, setting the stage for a deeper exploration of its use and legacy in subsequent chapters.

CHAPTER TWO

Early Navigational Tools and Techniques

Predecessors of the Sextant: Astrolabe, Quadrant, and Other Early Instruments

Before the sextant's advent revolutionized navigation, mariners relied on a variety of tools to chart their course across the vast and often perilous oceans. These early instruments, while groundbreaking for their time, had significant limitations that made precise navigation challenging. Understanding these tools provides valuable context for appreciating the advancements brought about by the sextant.

The Astrolabe

The astrolabe is one of the oldest known navigational instruments, with its origins tracing back to ancient Greece around 150 BC. The device was later refined by Islamic scholars and eventually introduced to Europe.

The mariner's astrolabe, specifically designed for navigation at sea, emerged in the late 15th century.

Structure and Function

- **Components**: The mariner's astrolabe typically consisted of a brass or bronze disk with a graduated scale around its circumference. A movable arm, called an alidade, was attached to the center of the disk.

- **Operation**: To measure the altitude of a celestial body, the navigator would sight the object along the alidade and read the angle from the scale. This angle, combined with the date and time of the observation, allowed the navigator to determine their latitude.

Limitations:

- **Accuracy**: The astrolabe's accuracy was often compromised by its exposure to the elements and the difficulty of steadying the device on a moving ship.

- **Ease of Use**: Its large and heavy structure made it cumbersome to use, especially in rough sea conditions.

The Quadrant

The quadrant, named for its quarter-circle shape, was another early navigational tool. It was simpler and more portable than the astrolabe, making it popular among sailors.

Structure and Function

- **Components**: A typical quadrant was made of wood or brass, with a 90-degree arc marked with a scale. A plumb line with a weight was attached to the vertex of the arc.

- **Operation**: The navigator would sight a celestial object along one edge of the quadrant and read the angle from the scale where the plumb line intersected it. This measurement provided the altitude of the object, which could be used to calculate latitude.

Limitations:

- **Environmental Sensitivity**: Like the astrolabe, the quadrant was affected by the ship's motion and the wind, which could sway the plumb line and affect readings.

- **Precision**: While more portable, the quadrant offered limited precision compared to later instruments.

The Cross-Staff

The cross-staff, also known as the Jacob's staff, was another tool used for determining the altitude of celestial bodies. It became widely used in the 16th century.

Structure and Function

- **Components**: The cross-staff consisted of a long, straight staff with a perpendicular cross-piece that could slide along its length.

- **Operation**: The navigator would hold
  the staff to their eye and slide the cross-
  piece until one end aligned with the
  horizon and the other with the celestial
  body. The position of the cross-piece
  along the staff indicated the angle of
  elevation.

Limitations:

- **Accuracy**: Measurements were often
  imprecise due to the difficulty of
  maintaining steady alignment.

- **Usage Difficulty**: The need to sight
  along the staff made it challenging to
  use, particularly in adverse weather
  conditions.

The Backstaff

Developed by English navigator John Davis in
the late 16th century, the backstaff addressed
some of the limitations of earlier instruments by
allowing navigators to measure the sun's
altitude without directly looking at it.

Structure and Function

- **Components**: The backstaff had a main staff and a series of arcs and vanes.

- **Operation**: The navigator would stand with their back to the sun, align the instrument's shadow vane with the horizon, and read the altitude from the arc where the shadow fell.

Limitations:

- **Complexity**: While more accurate for solar observations, the backstaff was more complex to use and required careful alignment and interpretation.

Navigational Challenges: Problems Faced by Early Sailors Without Precise Instruments

Navigating the open ocean has always been fraught with challenges. Before the development of precise instruments like the sextant, sailors faced numerous difficulties that often led to perilous journeys and disastrous outcomes.

Determining Latitude

Latitude, the measurement of distance north or south of the equator, was relatively easier to determine compared to longitude. Early navigators used the North Star (Polaris) in the Northern Hemisphere and the Southern Cross constellation in the Southern Hemisphere to estimate their latitude. Despite the availability of these celestial markers, achieving precise measurements was difficult with early tools.

Challenges:

- **Instrumental Limitations**: Instruments like the astrolabe and quadrant were susceptible to errors caused by the ship's movement, wind, and waves.

- **Environmental Conditions**: Cloudy skies, fog, and storms often obscured celestial objects, making consistent observations difficult.

- **Human Error**: Manual readings and calculations were prone to mistakes, especially under the stressful conditions of a sea voyage.

Determining Longitude

Longitude, the measurement of distance east or west of a prime meridian, posed a far greater challenge. Accurate determination of longitude required precise timekeeping, as the Earth rotates 15 degrees of longitude per hour.

Challenges:

- **Lack of Accurate Timekeeping**: Before the invention of reliable marine chronometers, sailors had no way to measure time accurately at sea. Pendulum clocks were ineffective due to the motion of the ship.

- **Celestial Navigation Limitations**: Methods such as dead reckoning, which involved estimating position based on speed and direction, were highly unreliable over long distances.

- **Distance Estimation**: Without accurate longitude, navigators had difficulty determining their precise east-west position, leading to navigation errors and potential shipwrecks.

Navigational Hazards

The lack of precise instruments compounded the inherent dangers of sea travel.

Challenges:

- **Unknown Waters**: Early explorers ventured into uncharted territories with little knowledge of hazards such as reefs, shoals, and dangerous currents.

- **Course Correction**: Inaccurate navigation made it difficult to correct course, leading to longer voyages and increased risk of running out of supplies.

- **Human and Environmental Factors**: Misjudgments in navigation could result in collisions, stranding, and conflicts with other vessels or coastal communities.

Evolution of Navigation: Transition from Celestial Navigation to the Use of the Sextant

The evolution of navigation from rudimentary tools to the precision of the sextant was a gradual process marked by significant milestones. This transition improved the safety and efficiency of maritime travel, facilitating global exploration and trade.

The Role of Celestial Navigation

Celestial navigation, the practice of determining position by observing celestial bodies, has been a cornerstone of maritime navigation for centuries. Early tools like the astrolabe and quadrant laid the groundwork for more precise instruments.

Key Practices:

- **Polaris for Latitude**: Navigators in the Northern Hemisphere used the altitude of Polaris to estimate their latitude. Polaris's position near the North Pole made it a reliable marker.

- **Solar Observations**: The sun's noon altitude was used to determine latitude by measuring its highest point in the sky. This practice required accurate tables of the sun's declination.

- **Lunar Distance Method**: This method involved measuring the angular distance between the moon and another celestial body. It was used to estimate longitude but required complex calculations and precise instruments.

The Advent of the Sextant

The development of the sextant in the 18th century addressed many of the limitations of earlier instruments, offering greater precision and ease of use.

Advantages:

- **Double-Reflecting Principle**: The sextant's use of two mirrors allowed for direct readings of angles up to 120 degrees, improving accuracy and reducing errors caused by the ship's movement.

- **Portability and Durability**: Made from brass or other durable materials, the sextant was robust and portable, suitable for use in various sea conditions.

- **Integration with Timekeeping**: The sextant's precision complemented the marine chronometer, enabling accurate determination of longitude through celestial observations.

Impact on Exploration and Trade

The sextant's introduction revolutionized maritime navigation, facilitating safer and more efficient sea voyages.

Key Impacts:

- **Expanded Exploration**: Accurate navigation enabled explorers to venture further into unknown territories with confidence. This period saw significant discoveries and detailed mapping of previously uncharted regions.

- **Global Trade**: Improved navigation routes reduced travel time and costs, boosting global trade and economic exchange. The ability to navigate open oceans efficiently led to the establishment of new trade routes.

- **Scientific Advancements**: The precision of the sextant contributed to scientific exploration, allowing for the collection of accurate data on geography, ocean currents, and weather patterns.

The Sextant in Modern Navigation

While modern electronic systems like GPS have largely supplanted traditional navigational instruments, the sextant remains a valuable tool for mariners.

Ongoing Relevance:

- **Backup Navigation**: Many sailors and navigators continue to learn and practice celestial navigation using the sextant as a backup in case of electronic failure.

- **Cultural Heritage**: The sextant symbolizes the ingenuity and skill of traditional navigation, preserving an important aspect of maritime history.

- **Educational Value**: Training in sextant use provides a deeper understanding of navigational principles and the challenges faced by early explorers.

The evolution of navigational tools from the astrolabe and quadrant to the sextant represents a remarkable journey of innovation and discovery. Each instrument played a crucial role in advancing maritime navigation, overcoming challenges, and paving the way for global exploration and trade. By understanding the history and function of these early tools, we gain a greater appreciation for the sextant's transformative impact on navigation and its enduring legacy in the maritime world.

This chapter has explored the predecessors of the sextant, the navigational challenges faced by early sailors, and the significant advancements that led to the sextant's development. As we move forward, we will delve deeper into the mechanics of the sextant, its practical use, and its continued relevance in the age of electronic navigation.

CHAPTER THREE

Key Figures in Nautical Cartography

Nautical cartography, the science and art of map-making for maritime navigation, has been shaped by the contributions of several key figures throughout history. These individuals not only advanced the field but also revolutionized navigation and exploration. This chapter focuses on three pivotal figures: John Harrison, whose inventions solved the longitude problem; Captain James Cook, who utilized the sextant in his groundbreaking voyages; and other significant navigators who made crucial contributions to nautical cartography.

John Harrison: Contributions to Solving the Longitude Problem

The Longitude Problem

For centuries, the inability to accurately determine longitude at sea was one of the greatest challenges in navigation.

While latitude could be determined relatively easily by measuring the angle of the sun or stars above the horizon, longitude required precise timekeeping. The Earth rotates 15 degrees of longitude per hour, meaning that knowing the exact time at a reference location (such as Greenwich) and comparing it to the local time at sea could provide a ship's longitude. However, pendulum clocks of the era were unreliable at sea due to the ship's motion and varying environmental conditions.

John Harrison's Early Life and Career

John Harrison was born on March 24, 1693, in Foulby, Yorkshire, England. A self-taught carpenter and clockmaker, Harrison developed a keen interest in precision timekeeping. By the early 1720s, he had constructed his first wooden clocks, which were notable for their accuracy. His talent for clockmaking would eventually lead him to tackle the longitude problem.

The Board of Longitude and Harrison's Quest

In 1714, the British government established the Board of Longitude, offering a £20,000 prize (equivalent to millions today) for a practical method of determining longitude at sea to within half a degree. Harrison was determined to win this prize.

1. **H1 (1735)**: Harrison's first marine chronometer, the H1, was a large, heavy clock designed to remain accurate despite the motion of a ship. It employed a system of counterweights and balances to negate the effects of a rolling ship. While innovative, it was not practical for widespread use.

2. **H2 (1741)**: Harrison refined his design with the H2, which improved on the stability and accuracy of the H1. However, it still faced challenges in maintaining precision over long voyages.

3. **H3 (1759)**: Harrison's third chronometer introduced bimetallic strips to compensate for temperature variations, a significant advancement in maintaining accuracy. Despite its innovations, the H3 was still not deemed practical.

4. **H4 (1761)**: The breakthrough came with the H4, a sea watch resembling a large pocket watch. The H4 was significantly smaller and more practical than its predecessors. It underwent rigorous sea trials, including a voyage to Jamaica, where it proved to be remarkably accurate, maintaining time within seconds over long distances.

Recognition and Impact

Despite initial skepticism and bureaucratic hurdles, Harrison's work was eventually recognized. In 1773, at the age of 80, he was awarded £10,000, and later an additional £8,750, by the Board of Longitude.

The success of Harrison's H4 and subsequent refinements by others paved the way for accurate marine chronometers, revolutionizing navigation by providing a reliable method to determine longitude at sea.

Harrison's contributions cannot be overstated. His inventions drastically reduced the risks of maritime travel, enabling safer and more precise navigation. His work laid the foundation for global exploration and trade, significantly impacting nautical cartography by allowing more accurate charting of sea routes.

Captain James Cook: Use of the Sextant in His Voyages and Its Impact on His Discoveries

Early Life and Naval Career

Captain James Cook was born on October 27, 1728, in Marton, Yorkshire, England. He joined the British merchant navy as a teenager and later enlisted in the Royal Navy. Cook quickly rose through the ranks due to his exceptional skills in navigation and cartography.

The First Voyage (1768-1771)

Cook's first voyage aboard the HMS Endeavour was commissioned by the Royal Society to observe the transit of Venus across the Sun, which was crucial for determining the Earth-Sun distance. However, a secondary mission was to seek the unknown southern continent (Terra Australis).

Use of the Sextant

- **Precision Navigation**: Cook's voyage was among the first to benefit from the recently improved sextant. The instrument allowed Cook to determine latitude and longitude with unprecedented accuracy.

- **Charting New Territories**: Cook meticulously charted the coastlines of New Zealand and eastern Australia, making detailed maps that remained in use for centuries. His observations debunked the myth of Terra Australis and provided the first accurate maps of these regions.

The Second Voyage (1772-1775)

Cook's second voyage aboard the HMS Resolution aimed to further explore the southern hemisphere and verify the existence of Terra Australis.

Navigational Achievements:

- **Antarctic Circle**: Cook and his crew crossed the Antarctic Circle, the first known Europeans to do so, proving that if a southern continent existed, it was not as large as previously thought.

- **Sextant Use**: The sextant's accuracy allowed Cook to navigate through the ice-filled southern oceans, contributing to detailed charts of the region.

The Third Voyage (1776-1779)

Cook's final voyage sought the Northwest Passage, a hypothesized sea route connecting the Atlantic and Pacific Oceans.

Key Discoveries:

- **Hawaii**: Cook's detailed charts and navigational skills led to the discovery of the Hawaiian Islands, which he named the Sandwich Islands.

- **Bering Strait**: Cook attempted to navigate the Bering Strait, but was turned back by ice. His charts of the North American northwest coast were highly accurate and valuable to future explorers.

Legacy and Impact

Captain James Cook's use of the sextant and his contributions to nautical cartography were monumental. His accurate maps and charts facilitated future explorations and trade routes. Cook's meticulous observations and recordings set new standards for maritime navigation, emphasizing the importance of precise instruments like the sextant in exploration. His voyages expanded the known world, significantly contributing to the global understanding of geography.

Other Pioneers: Brief Profiles of Other Significant Navigators and Their Use of the Sextant

While John Harrison and Captain James Cook are among the most renowned figures in nautical cartography, many other navigators made significant contributions to the field. This section profiles a few of these pioneers and highlights their use of the sextant in advancing maritime navigation.

Ferdinand Magellan (1480-1521)

Contributions:

- **Circumnavigation**: Magellan's expedition (1519-1522) was the first to circumnavigate the globe, proving that the Earth was round and much larger than previously thought.

- **Navigational Techniques**: Although Magellan did not use a sextant (it had not yet been invented), his voyages relied heavily on celestial navigation, using the astrolabe and quadrant.

Sir Francis Drake (1540-1596)

Contributions:

- **Circumnavigation**: Drake was the second person to lead an expedition that circumnavigated the globe (1577-1580). His detailed maps and charts of the Pacific Ocean were invaluable to future explorers.

- **Innovation**: Drake's navigational techniques, including dead reckoning and celestial navigation, laid the groundwork for future advancements, including the use of the sextant.

Edmond Halley (1656-1742)

Contributions:

- **Scientific Voyages**: Halley, an astronomer best known for Halley's Comet, conducted several voyages to improve nautical cartography and understand magnetic declination.

- **Navigational Instruments**: Halley's work in refining navigational instruments, including the sextant, helped improve the accuracy of sea charts.

George Vancouver (1757-1798)

Contributions:

- **Pacific Northwest Exploration**: Vancouver's detailed surveys and maps of the Pacific Northwest (1791-1795) were some of the most accurate of their time.

- **Sextant Use**: Vancouver extensively used the sextant to chart the complex coastlines of modern-day British Columbia, Washington, and Alaska, contributing to the region's nautical cartography.

Nathaniel Bowditch (1773-1838)

Contributions:

- **"The American Practical Navigator"**: Bowditch's book, first published in 1802, revolutionized maritime navigation by compiling and standardizing navigational techniques and astronomical tables.

- **Advocacy for the Sextant**: Bowditch's work emphasized the importance of the sextant in celestial navigation, making the instrument an essential tool for mariners.

Matthew Flinders (1774-1814)

Contributions:

- **Mapping Australia**: Flinders was the first to circumnavigate Australia (1801-1803) and confirm it as a continent. His detailed maps and charts were crucial for future navigation.

- **Sextant Use**: Flinders relied heavily on the sextant to produce accurate coastal surveys, which remain foundational in Australian nautical cartography.

The field of nautical cartography has been shaped by the remarkable contributions of numerous key figures. John Harrison's invention of the marine chronometer solved the longitude problem, revolutionizing navigation. Captain James Cook's use of the sextant in his voyages led to groundbreaking discoveries and the creation of highly accurate maps. Other significant navigators, including Ferdinand Magellan, Sir Francis Drake, Edmond Halley, George Vancouver, Nathaniel Bowditch, and Matthew Flinders, also made invaluable contributions to maritime exploration and cartography.

These pioneers advanced the science and art of navigation, enabling safer and more precise sea travel. Their legacy endures in the accurate charts and maps that continue to guide mariners today. Understanding their contributions provides a deeper appreciation for the sextant's role in nautical history and its lasting impact on global exploration and trade.

The Mechanics of the Sextant

The sextant is a marvel of precision engineering, designed to measure the angle between two visible objects. This chapter delves into the mechanics of the sextant, providing a comprehensive understanding of its components, how it works, and how to care for and maintain this crucial navigational instrument.

Components

A sextant comprises several key components, each playing a vital role in its operation. Understanding these parts is essential for using the instrument effectively and maintaining its accuracy.

Frame

The frame is the backbone of the sextant, providing the structural integrity and stability necessary for accurate measurements. Typically made from brass, aluminum, or other durable materials, the frame must withstand the harsh conditions of a marine environment.

- **Types of Frames**: There are generally two types of frames: open-frame and solid-frame. Open-frame sextants are lighter and less susceptible to temperature-induced expansion or contraction. Solid-frame sextants are heavier but offer greater protection against mechanical damage.

- **Arc**: The frame features a graduated arc marked with degrees and minutes, ranging from $0°$ to about $140°$, although most measurements are taken within the $60°$ range. This arc is crucial for determining the angle of elevation or depression between two objects.

Mirrors

The sextant uses two mirrors to bring the images of celestial objects and the horizon into the same field of view, allowing the observer to measure the angle between them.

- **Index Mirror**: Attached to the index arm, the index mirror reflects the image of the celestial object. Its position changes as the index arm moves along the arc.

- **Horizon Mirror**: Mounted on the frame, the horizon mirror is partially silvered. This mirror reflects the horizon, allowing the observer to see both the horizon and the reflected celestial object simultaneously.

- **Alignment and Adjustment**: Proper alignment and adjustment of these mirrors are critical for accurate measurements. Most sextants come with adjustment screws to fine-tune the mirrors' positions.

Index Arm

The index arm is a movable arm that rotates around the pivot point of the frame. It carries the index mirror and a vernier scale or micrometer drum used to read precise angles.

- **Micrometer Drum/Vernier Scale**: The micrometer drum allows fine adjustments and precise readings of angles, typically accurate to the nearest tenth of a minute. Older sextants use a vernier scale for this purpose.

- **Clamping Mechanism**: The index arm can be clamped in place once the desired angle is roughly set, allowing for fine adjustments with the micrometer drum.

Telescope

The sextant includes a small, low-power telescope that enhances the observer's ability to see the celestial object and horizon clearly.

- **Types of Telescopes**: Sextants may use either a Galilean or a Keplerian (inverting) telescope. Galilean telescopes provide an upright image and are simpler to use, while Keplerian telescopes offer higher magnification and better resolution but invert the image.

- **Mounting**: The telescope is mounted parallel to the frame, aligned with the horizon mirror. It can be adjusted for focus and alignment to ensure both the horizon and the celestial object are sharp and clear.

Other Components

- **Filters**: Sextants often come with filters or shades to reduce the glare of the sun or other bright celestial objects, protecting the observer's eyes and improving visibility.

- **Sighting Mechanism**: Some sextants include a peep sight or sighting tube for aligning the instrument with the horizon and celestial object before using the telescope.

How It Works

The sextant operates on the principle of double reflection, enabling the measurement of the angle between two objects by bringing their images into coincidence. Here's a step-by-step explanation of how the sextant works:

Measuring Angles

1. **Initial Setup**:

    - **Hold the Sextant**: Hold the sextant vertically by its handle with the frame's arc facing you.

Ensure the index arm is unclamped and can move freely.

- **Look Through the Telescope**: Look through the telescope or sighting mechanism, aligning the horizon in the field of view.

2. **Aligning the Celestial Object**:

- **Adjust the Index Arm**: Move the index arm slowly to bring the image of the celestial object (e.g., the sun or a star) into view via the index mirror.

- **Coincide with the Horizon**: Continue adjusting the index arm until the reflected image of the celestial object appears to touch or align with the horizon visible through the unsilvered part of the horizon mirror.

3. **Fine Adjustment**:

- **Clamp the Index Arm**: Once the images are roughly aligned, clamp the index arm in place to prevent large movements.

- **Use the Micrometer Drum**: Fine-tune the position of the index arm using the micrometer drum, bringing the images into precise coincidence.

4. **Reading the Angle**:

- **Read the Vernier Scale/Micrometer Drum**: The angle between the celestial object and the horizon is read directly from the arc, using the vernier scale or micrometer drum for precise measurement. This angle is known as the sextant angle or altitude.

Practical Example: Measuring the Sun's Altitude

1. **Safety First**: Attach the appropriate filters to protect your eyes from the sun's glare.

2. **Initial Positioning**: Set the sextant to zero and hold it vertically. Look through the telescope and align the horizon in the field of view.

3. **Adjust the Index Arm**: Slowly move the index arm to bring the sun's image into view.

4. **Align the Sun and Horizon**: Adjust the index arm until the lower edge of the sun appears to touch the horizon.

5. **Fine-Tuning**: Clamp the index arm and use the micrometer drum for precise alignment, ensuring the sun's lower edge just touches the horizon.

6. **Record the Reading**: Read the sextant angle from the arc and micrometer drum. This angle, combined with the exact time of observation, allows for the determination of the observer's latitude.

Care and Maintenance

Proper care and maintenance are essential to ensure the sextant remains accurate and reliable. Here are guidelines for preserving and maintaining the instrument:

Cleaning

- **General Cleaning**: Wipe the frame, index arm, and mirrors with a soft, lint-free cloth after each use to remove salt, dirt, and fingerprints.

- **Mirrors and Lenses**: Use lens cleaning solutions and microfiber cloths to clean the mirrors and telescope lenses. Avoid using harsh chemicals or abrasive materials that can scratch or damage the optical surfaces.

Storage

- **Protective Case**: Store the sextant in a sturdy, padded case to protect it from physical damage and environmental factors. Many sextants come with custom cases designed for this purpose.

- **Dry Environment**: Keep the sextant in a dry, cool environment to prevent corrosion and mold growth. Avoid exposing the instrument to extreme temperatures or humidity.

Calibration and Adjustment

- **Regular Checks**: Periodically check the alignment and calibration of the sextant. Small misalignments can lead to significant errors in measurements.

- **Adjusting Mirrors**: Use the adjustment screws to align the index and horizon mirrors. Many sextants include a tool or key specifically for this purpose.

- **Professional Servicing**: If the sextant requires major adjustments or repairs, consider having it serviced by a professional. Specialized technicians can recalibrate the instrument to ensure optimal accuracy.

Handling

- **Careful Handling**: Handle the sextant with care, avoiding rough or sudden movements that could knock it out of alignment.

- **Avoiding Contamination**: Keep the sextant free from oils, grease, and other contaminants that can affect its mechanical and optical components.

Advanced Techniques and Tips

To master the use of the sextant, it's helpful to understand some advanced techniques and practical tips:

Index Error Correction

Index error occurs when the index mirror and horizon mirror are not perfectly parallel when the index arm is set to zero. This error can be corrected by:

- **Measuring the Sun's Diameter**: Measure the angle between the upper and lower limbs of the sun. The difference from the expected value (approximately 32 arcminutes) is the index error.

- **Adjusting for Index Error**: Apply the correction by adding or subtracting the index error from all sextant readings.

Taking Sights at Sea

- **Steady the Sextant**: On a moving ship, it can be challenging to keep the sextant steady. Practice bracing yourself against a stable part of the ship and take multiple readings to average out the motion effects.

- **Timing**: Accurate timing is crucial for celestial navigation. Use a reliable marine chronometer or a GPS time signal to record the exact time of each sight.

Night Observations

- **Celestial Navigation at Night**: Stars and planets provide excellent reference points for night observations. Ensure the sextant's telescope and mirrors are properly aligned and clean to enhance visibility in low light conditions.

- **Star Charts**: Use star charts or navigation apps to identify celestial objects and their positions for accurate sightings.

The sextant, with its intricate mechanics and precision, remains a testament to human ingenuity in navigation. By understanding its components, learning how it works, and practicing proper care and maintenance, mariners can harness the sextant's full potential for accurate celestial navigation. Whether used in historical exploration or as a backup to modern electronic systems, the sextant continues to be a vital tool for navigators worldwide. This chapter has provided a detailed exploration of the sextant's mechanics, equipping you with the knowledge to use and maintain this indispensable instrument effectively.

Practical Use of the Sextant

In this chapter, we will explore the practical use of the sextant in detail. By the end of this chapter, you should be able to confidently take a celestial reading, calculate your position (latitude and longitude), and troubleshoot common mistakes. We will break this down into three main sections: taking a reading, calculating position, and common mistakes.

Taking a Reading

Taking a reading with a sextant involves several precise steps. These are the comprehensive, step-by-step guide:

Step 1: Prepare the Sextant

1. **Inspect the Instrument**:

   - **Clean the Mirrors and Telescope**: Ensure the mirrors and telescope are free of dust and smudges.

- **Check the Arc and Index Arm**: Verify that the arc and index arm are clean and move smoothly.

- **Zero the Sextant**: Set the index arm to 0° and check for any index error by observing the horizon through the telescope. If the horizon line appears unbroken and continuous, there is no index error. If not, note the error for correction later.

2. **Set Up for Observation**:

- **Filters**: If observing the sun, attach the appropriate sun filters to protect your eyes.

- **Telescope Adjustment**: Ensure the telescope is focused correctly for clear viewing of both the horizon and celestial object.

Step 2: Sight the Celestial Object

1. **Initial Position**:

   - Hold the sextant vertically by the handle. Look through the telescope or sighting mechanism to locate the horizon.

2. **Aligning the Celestial Object**:

   - Move the index arm slowly to bring the celestial object (e.g., the sun, moon, or a star) into the field of view via the index mirror.

3. **Coincide with the Horizon**:

   - Adjust the index arm until the reflected image of the celestial object touches or aligns with the horizon visible through the unsilvered part of the horizon mirror.

Step 3: Fine Adjustment

1. **Clamp the Index Arm**:

   - Once the images are roughly aligned, clamp the index arm in place to prevent large movements.

2. **Use the Micrometer Drum**:

   - Fine-tune the position of the index arm using the micrometer drum, bringing the images into precise coincidence. For the sun, align the lower edge (lower limb) or upper edge (upper limb) with the horizon.

Step 4: Record the Reading

1. **Read the Vernier Scale/Micrometer Drum**:

   - Read the sextant angle from the arc using the vernier scale or micrometer drum for precise measurement. This angle is known as the sextant altitude (Hs).

2. **Note the Exact Time**:

- Record the exact time of the observation using a reliable time source, such as a chronometer or GPS.

3. **Apply Corrections**:

- Apply any necessary corrections for index error, dip (height of eye above sea level), and refraction. These corrections are found in nautical almanacs and tables.

Calculating Position

Once you have taken a sextant reading, the next step is to calculate your position, specifically your latitude and longitude.

Determining Latitude

Latitude is determined using the altitude of the sun at local noon (meridian passage) or the altitude of a star.

1. **Noon Sight Method**:

    - **Take the Noon Sight**: At local noon, when the sun reaches its highest point in the sky (culmination), take a reading of its altitude. This is the solar altitude at noon.

    - **Record Time and Altitude**: Note the exact time and the corrected sextant altitude.

    - **Calculate Declination**: Use the nautical almanac to find the sun's declination (δ) for the date and time of observation.

    - **Calculate Latitude (φ):**

$$\varphi = 90° - Hs + \delta$$

    - Where Hs is the corrected sextant altitude.

2. **Star Sight Method**:

- **Take a Star Sight**: At a known time, measure the altitude of a known star.

- **Record Time and Altitude**: Note the exact time and the corrected sextant altitude.

- **Use Almanac and Tables**: Use the nautical almanac and sight reduction tables to calculate latitude from the star sight.

Determining Longitude

Longitude is determined by comparing the local time of an observed celestial event with the time of the same event at a known reference location (e.g., Greenwich Mean Time - GMT).

1. **Measure Local Time**:

- **Take a Time Sight**: Measure the altitude of the sun or a star and note the exact local time of the observation.

2. **Determine Greenwich Time**:

- **Reference Time**: Use the nautical almanac to find the GMT of the same event (e.g., sunrise, noon, or a specific star sighting).

3. **Calculate Time Difference**:

- **Time Difference**: Calculate the time difference between the local time and GMT.

- **Convert to Degrees**: Convert the time difference into degrees (15° per hour). If the local time is ahead of GMT, you are east of Greenwich. If behind, you are west.

4. **Calculate Longitude (λ):**

$$\lambda = \text{Time Difference}\,(h \ldots$$

$$\ldots) \times 15° \quad \lambda = TimeDifference(hours) \times 15°$$

Practical Example: Latitude and Longitude Calculation

Example: Calculating Latitude at Noon

1. **Observed Altitude (Hs):** Suppose you measured the sun's lower limb altitude at local noon as 45° 30'.

2. **Corrections:** Apply corrections for index error (+1'), dip (-2'), and refraction (-1'). The total correction is -2'.

    - Corrected Sextant Altitude (Ho): 45° 30' - 2' = 45° 28'.

3. **Declination (δ)**: From the nautical almanac, find the sun's declination on the date of observation, e.g., +15° 20'.

4. **Calculate Latitude (φ)**:

❖=90°−45°28′+15°20′=59°52′❖φ=90°−45°28′+15°20′=59°52′N

Example: Calculating Longitude from a Morning Sight

1. **Observed Altitude (Hs)**: Suppose you measured the sun's lower limb altitude at 09:00 local time as 20° 15'.

2. **Corrections**: Apply corrections for index error (+1'), dip (-2'), and refraction (-1'). The total correction is -2'.

    - Corrected Sextant Altitude (Ho): 20° 15' - 2' = 20° 13'.

3. **Greenwich Time (GMT)**: Use the nautical almanac to find the GMT of the event. Suppose the GMT for this altitude on the same date is 12:00.

4. **Local Time Difference**: Local time is 09:00. The time difference is 3 hours (12:00 - 09:00).

5. **Convert to Degrees**:

��������������$=3\times15°=45°$

$TimeDifference=3\times15°=45°$

6. **Calculate Longitude (λ)**:

    - If local time is behind GMT, longitude is west. Hence,

�$=45°$�$\lambda=45°W$

Common Mistakes and Troubleshooting

Using a sextant can be challenging, and several common mistakes can affect the accuracy of your readings. These are some tips for troubleshooting:

Common Mistakes

1. **Incorrect Index Error Correction**:

   - Ensure you correctly determine and apply the index error. Misjudging this correction can lead to significant errors in altitude measurements.

2. **Misaligned Mirrors**:

   - Regularly check and align the index and horizon mirrors. Misalignment can cause incorrect sightings and inaccurate angles.

3. **Poor Horizon Visibility**:

   - When the horizon is unclear due to fog, haze, or low light, your readings can be compromised. Use a clear day and a stable platform for observations.

4. **Timing Errors**:

   - Accurate timing is crucial. Ensure your timepiece is reliable and synchronized with a known standard, such as GMT.

5. **Incorrect Altitude Corrections**:

   - Apply all necessary corrections, including dip, refraction, semi-diameter (for sun or moon), and parallax (for moon). Missing or incorrect corrections can lead to errors.

Troubleshooting Tips

1. **Practice and Familiarity**:

   - Regular practice improves familiarity with the sextant and reduces errors. Practice taking sights on land before using the sextant at sea.

2. **Multiple Readings**:

   - Take multiple readings and average them to mitigate the effects of ship motion and observational errors.

3. **Stable Platform**:

   - On a moving vessel, brace yourself and the sextant against a stable part of the ship. This reduces the impact of the vessel's motion on your readings.

4. **Verify with Known Positions**:

   - Verify your sextant readings and calculated positions with known locations or electronic navigation systems whenever possible.

5. **Record Keeping**:

   - Keep detailed records of each sight, including date, time, observed altitude, corrections applied, and calculated position.

This helps identify patterns and correct recurring errors.

The practical use of the sextant is an essential skill for celestial navigation. By following the step-by-step guide to taking a reading, accurately calculating your position, and understanding common mistakes and troubleshooting methods, you can harness the full potential of this remarkable instrument. Whether used as a primary navigation tool or a backup to modern electronic systems, the sextant remains an invaluable device for mariners. Through practice and meticulous attention to detail, you can achieve precise and reliable navigation using the sextant.

CHAPTER SIX

Celestial Navigation Techniques

Celestial navigation, the practice of using celestial bodies to determine one's position at sea, has been a cornerstone of maritime exploration for centuries. This chapter explores three primary celestial navigation techniques: using the sun to find noon and calculate latitude, using the stars for nighttime navigation, and the lunar distance method for calculating longitude. Each section will provide detailed teaching explanations and step-by-step procedures to master these techniques.

Using the Sun: Finding Noon and Calculating Latitude

The sun is the most reliable celestial object for navigation because it is visible during the day and its position changes predictably. Using the sun to find local noon and calculate latitude is a fundamental skill in celestial navigation.

Finding Local Noon

Local noon, also known as meridian passage, is the moment when the sun reaches its highest point in the sky, directly above the observer's meridian. This point, known as solar noon, does not necessarily coincide with 12:00 on a clock due to the equation of time and the observer's longitude.

Steps to Find Local Noon:

1. **Prepare the Sextant**:

   - Ensure the sextant is clean and properly adjusted.

   - Attach the appropriate sun filters to protect your eyes.

2. **Take Preliminary Readings**:

   - About 30 minutes before the estimated local noon, start taking regular sextant readings of the sun's altitude.

- Record the altitude and exact time of each reading.

3. **Continue Observations**:

   - As you approach local noon, take more frequent readings (every 1-2 minutes). The sun's altitude will increase until it peaks at local noon.

   - Once the altitude starts to decrease, you've passed local noon.

4. **Identify Local Noon**:

   - Local noon is identified as the time at which the sun reaches its maximum altitude.

   - Record this time and the corresponding altitude.

Calculating Latitude at Local Noon

To calculate latitude using the sun at local noon, you need the sun's declination (δ) for the date

of observation and the corrected altitude (Ho)
measured at local noon.

Steps to Calculate Latitude:

1. **Determine Corrected Altitude (Ho):**

   - Take the observed altitude (Hs) at
     local noon.

   - Apply necessary corrections:

     - Index error (IE)

     - Dip (height of eye above
       sea level)

     - Refraction

     - Semi-diameter (if
       measuring the sun's lower
       limb)

   - Corrected altitude (Ho) = Hs + IE
     - Dip - Refraction + Semi-
     diameter

2. **Find the Sun's Declination (δ)**:

- Use the nautical almanac to find the sun's declination for the exact date and time of observation.

3. **Calculate Latitude (φ)**:

- Use the following formula:

$$\phi = 90° - Ho + \delta$$

- If the declination and observed altitude are on the same side of the equator (both north or both south), add the declination.

- If they are on opposite sides, subtract the declination.

Example Calculation:

1. **Observed Altitude (Hs)**: 60° 30'

2. **Corrections**:

- Index error: +2'

- Dip: -2'

- Refraction: -1'

- Semi-diameter: +16' (for lower limb)

3. **Corrected Altitude (Ho)**:

$$Ho=60°30'+2'-2'-1'+16'=60°45' \quad Ho=60°30'+2'-2'-1'+16'=60°45'$$

4. **Sun's Declination (δ)**: +20° 00' (north)

5. **Calculate Latitude (φ)**:

$$\phi=90°-60°45'+20°00'=49°15' \quad \phi=90°-60°45'+20°00'=49°15'N$$

Using the Stars: Techniques for Nighttime Navigation

Stars are excellent navigational aids due to their fixed positions in the sky. Nighttime navigation using stars requires identifying specific stars and their positions relative to the observer's horizon.

Identifying Navigational Stars

Navigational stars are prominent stars used in celestial navigation. The International Astronomical Union (IAU) lists 57 navigational stars. These stars are bright, easily recognizable, and distributed evenly across the sky.

Steps to Identify Navigational Stars:

1. **Use a Star Chart**:

    - Star charts or planispheres help identify stars based on the observer's location and time of year.

2. **Learn Constellations**:

    - Recognizing constellations helps locate navigational stars within them. For example, Polaris is part of the Ursa Minor constellation.

3. **Use a Star Finder or App**:

    - Modern star-finding apps can help identify stars by pointing a device at the sky.

Measuring Altitude and Azimuth of Stars

1. **Prepare the Sextant**:

  - Ensure the sextant is clean, calibrated, and focused.

  - Align the telescope and mirrors for clear visibility.

2. **Take a Star Sight**:

  - Select a navigational star and measure its altitude above the horizon using the sextant.

  - Record the exact time of the sighting.

3. **Determine Azimuth**:

  - Azimuth is the star's direction relative to true north. Use a compass or azimuth tables to determine the azimuth.

4. **Correct the Altitude**:

  - Apply necessary corrections for index error, dip, and refraction to the observed altitude (Hs) to obtain the true altitude (Ho).

Calculating Position Using Star Sights

1. **Determine Local Hour Angle (LHA)**:

    - The Local Hour Angle (LHA) of a star is the angle measured westward from the local meridian to the star's hour circle.

    - Calculate LHA using Greenwich Hour Angle (GHA) and the observer's longitude (λ):

$$LHA = GHA - \lambda$$

    - If LHA is negative, add 360° to get a positive angle.

2. **Use Sight Reduction Tables**:

    - Sight reduction tables (e.g., HO 249 or HO 229) help convert the star's altitude and azimuth into a position line.

3. **Plot the Position Line**:

    - Plot the position line on a nautical chart. Multiple position lines from different stars intersect at the observer's position.

Example Calculation:

1. **Star**: Altair

2. **Observed Altitude (Hs)**: 35° 20'

3. **Time of Observation**: 22:00 GMT

4. **Corrections**:

   - Index error: +1'

   - Dip: -3'

   - Refraction: -2'

5. **Corrected Altitude (Ho)**:

$$\diamond\;\diamond = 35°20'+1'-3'-2'=35°16' \quad Ho=35°20'+1'-3'-2'=35°16'$$

6. **GHA (from almanac)**: 150°

7. **Observer's Longitude (λ)**: 60° W

8. **Calculate LHA**:

$$\diamond\;\diamond\;\diamond = 150°-(-60°)=150°+60°=210° \quad LHA=150°-(-60°)=150°+60°=210°$$

9. **Use Sight Reduction Tables**:

- Find the intercept and azimuth for Altair using the LHA and Ho.

10. **Plot Position Line**:

- Plot the azimuth and intercept on the chart to determine the position line.

The Lunar Distance Method: Calculating Longitude

The lunar distance method involves measuring the angular distance between the moon and another celestial object (e.g., a star or planet). This method was historically significant for determining longitude before the advent of accurate marine chronometers.

Principles of Lunar Distance

The moon moves quickly relative to the background stars, and its position can be predicted accurately. By measuring the angle between the moon and a fixed star and knowing the exact time, navigators could determine Greenwich Time and thus their longitude.

Steps to Use the Lunar Distance Method:

1. **Prepare the Sextant**:

   - Ensure the sextant is clean, calibrated, and focused.

   - Attach any necessary filters for observing the moon.

2. **Measure the Lunar Distance**:

   - Select a celestial object near the moon (e.g., a bright star or planet).

   - Measure the angular distance between the moon's limb and the celestial object using the sextant.

- Record the exact time of the measurement.

3. **Correct the Observed Distance**:

   - Apply corrections for index error, semi-diameter, and parallax.

4. **Use Nautical Almanac**:

   - Use the nautical almanac to find the predicted lunar distance for the recorded time and date.

5. **Determine Greenwich Time**:

   - Compare the observed lunar distance with the predicted distances in the almanac to determine the exact Greenwich Time.

6. **Calculate Longitude**:

- Calculate the time difference between local time and Greenwich Time.

- Convert this time difference into degrees (15° per hour).

Example Calculation:

1. **Observed Lunar Distance**: 35° 30'

2. **Time of Observation**: 12:00 local time

3. **Corrections**:

    - Index error: +2'

    - Semi-diameter: +16'

    - Parallax: -5'

4. **Corrected Lunar Distance**:

Corrected Distance=35°30′+2′+16′−5′=35°43′C
orrected Distance=35°30′+2′+16′−5′=35°43′

5. **Predicted Distance (from almanac)**:
   35° 43' at 15:00 GMT

6. **Determine Greenwich Time**:

- The observed distance matches
  the almanac distance at 15:00
  GMT.

7. **Calculate Local Time Difference**:

- Local time: 12:00

- Time difference: 3 hours

8. **Convert to Degrees**:

Longitude=3×15°=45°Longitude=3×15°=45°

- Since local time is behind GMT,
  longitude is 45° W.

Celestial navigation techniques provide a reliable method for determining one's position at sea. Using the sun to find noon and calculate latitude, employing stars for nighttime navigation, and applying the lunar distance method for longitude calculations are essential skills for any navigator. By mastering these techniques, mariners can ensure accurate and dependable navigation, even without modern electronic aids. This chapter has provided detailed, step-by-step explanations to equip you with the knowledge and skills needed for proficient celestial navigation. Through practice and careful observation, you can achieve precision in your navigational endeavors.

CHAPTER SEVEN

Mapping the Oceans

Mapping the oceans is a monumental task that has been undertaken by brave explorers and meticulous cartographers over centuries. This chapter delves into the surveying techniques employed by early oceanographers and navigators, the processes of creating nautical charts from sextant readings, and a detailed examination of major expeditions that significantly advanced our understanding of the world's oceans.

Surveying Techniques: Methods Used by Early Oceanographers and Navigators

Early oceanographic surveys were fundamental in mapping the vast, uncharted waters of the globe. These surveys were often carried out using rudimentary tools and methods that, despite their simplicity, laid the groundwork for modern oceanography.

Early Surveying Instruments

1. **Lead Line**:

   - **Description**: A simple yet effective tool consisting of a long rope with a lead weight at one end. The weight often had a hollow base that could capture seabed samples.

   - **Use**: Sailors would lower the lead line until it hit the seabed, then measure the length of the line to determine water depth. Seabed samples captured in the hollow base provided information on the seabed's composition.

2. **Log Line**:

   - **Description**: A rope with knots tied at regular intervals, attached to a wooden board.

   - **Use**: The log line was thrown overboard, and the number of knots that passed through the sailor's hands in a given time indicated the ship's speed.

3. **Astrolabe**:

   - **Description**: An ancient instrument used to measure the altitude of celestial bodies.

   - **Use**: By measuring the angle of the sun or a star above the horizon, sailors could estimate their latitude.

4. **Quadrant**:

- **Description**: A quarter-circle panel with a plumb line used to measure angles.

- **Use**: The quadrant was used to measure the altitude of the sun or stars, providing latitude information.

Surveying Methods

1. **Dead Reckoning**:

   - **Principle**: Estimating a ship's current position by using a previously determined position and advancing that position based upon known or estimated speeds over elapsed time and course.

- **Limitations**: Subject to cumulative errors due to inaccurate speed estimates, compass errors, and currents.

2. **Celestial Navigation**:

   - **Principle**: Using the positions of celestial bodies (sun, moon, stars, and planets) to determine one's position on Earth.

   - **Technique**: Involves measuring the altitude of celestial objects using instruments like the sextant and applying these measurements to nautical almanacs to calculate latitude and longitude.

3. **Soundings**:

   - **Principle**: Measuring water depth to understand underwater topography.

   - **Technique**: Repeatedly using the lead line to take depth measurements and recording these on a chart.

4. **Triangulation**:

- **Principle**: Determining the location of a point by forming triangles to it from known points.

- **Technique**: Measuring angles from two known points on shore to a third point on land or sea.

Creating Nautical Charts: How Sextant Readings Were Translated into Maps and Charts

Nautical charts are essential tools for navigation, providing detailed information about coastlines, sea depths, and hazards. The process of creating these charts from sextant readings and other measurements was labor-intensive and required precision.

Steps in Creating Nautical Charts

1. **Data Collection**:

   - **Sextant Readings**: Collecting precise angles between celestial bodies and the horizon.

   - **Soundings**: Measuring water depths at various points using lead lines.

   - **Shoreline Surveys**: Mapping the coastlines using triangulation and other techniques.

2. **Data Processing**:

   - **Calculation of Positions**: Using sextant readings to determine latitude and longitude.

   - **Correction of Errors**: Applying corrections for index error, dip, and refraction to the raw sextant data.

3. **Chart Compilation**:

- **Plotting Positions**: Marking calculated positions on a chart using a grid system based on latitude and longitude.

- **Drawing Coastlines**: Adding details of the coastline from shoreline surveys.

- **Depth Markings**: Indicating water depths at various points based on soundings.

4. **Detailing and Annotation**:

- **Navigation Hazards**: Marking rocks, reefs, and other hazards.

- **Additional Information**: Including tidal information, magnetic variations, and sailing directions.

Example of Chart Creation: Captain James Cook's Endeavors

1. **Surveying Techniques**:

- Captain Cook used lead lines extensively for soundings to map underwater topography.

- He employed the sextant for celestial navigation to fix precise positions.

2. **Chart Creation**:

- Cook meticulously recorded his findings and plotted them on charts, which included detailed observations of coastlines and sea depths.

- His charts were renowned for their accuracy and comprehensiveness, greatly enhancing maritime navigation.

Major Expeditions: Detailed Look at Significant Mapping Voyages

Several expeditions played crucial roles in the mapping of the world's oceans. These voyages not only provided detailed nautical charts but also expanded our understanding of oceanography and geography.

Captain James Cook's Voyages

1. **First Voyage (1768-1771)**:

    - **Objective**: Observe the transit of Venus and explore the South Pacific.

    - **Achievements**: Cook mapped New Zealand and the east coast of Australia, providing the first accurate charts of these regions.

    - **Techniques**: Used sextant readings for precise positioning and lead lines for soundings.

Second Voyage (1772-1775):

    - **Objective**: Search for the hypothetical southern continent (Terra Australis).

    - **Achievements**: Cook crossed the Antarctic Circle and disproved the existence of Terra Australis. He also mapped parts of the Pacific, including Tonga and Easter Island.

- **Techniques**: Employed advanced surveying techniques, including the use of the chronometer for accurate longitude measurements.

2. **Third Voyage (1776-1780)**:

- **Objective**: Find the Northwest Passage.

- **Achievements**: Cook charted the west coast of North America from California to the Bering Strait and numerous Pacific islands.

- **Techniques**: Continued to use celestial navigation and detailed shoreline surveys.

The Challenger Expedition (1872-1876)

1. **Objective**: Conduct a scientific investigation of the world's oceans.

2. **Achievements**:

- Mapped the ocean floor, discovering the Mid-Atlantic Ridge and the Mariana Trench.

- Collected extensive biological, chemical, and physical data about the oceans.

3. **Techniques**:

- Used deep-sea soundings to map underwater topography.

- Conducted systematic water sampling and dredging for marine specimens.

The United States Exploring Expedition (1838-1842)

1. **Objective**: Explore and survey the Pacific Ocean and surrounding lands.

2. **Achievements**:

- Mapped over 280 islands in the Pacific and charted the coast of Antarctica.

- Collected vast amounts of scientific data and specimens, leading to significant contributions in geology, botany, and anthropology.

3. **Techniques**:

   - Employed celestial navigation and lead lines for accurate charting.

   - Used triangulation to map islands and coastlines.

The Voyage of the Beagle (1831-1836)

1. **Objective**: Conduct a hydrographic survey of the southern coasts of South America.

2. **Achievements**:

   - Charles Darwin's observations during this voyage led to his theory of evolution.

   - Produced detailed charts of the South American coast and several Pacific islands.

3. **Techniques**:

- Used sextant readings and chronometers for precise positioning.

- Conducted detailed surveys of coastal regions and inland areas.

The history of mapping the oceans is a testament to human ingenuity, perseverance, and the relentless pursuit of knowledge.

Early oceanographers and navigators employed a variety of surveying techniques, often with rudimentary instruments, to chart the vast and uncharted waters. Their efforts laid the groundwork for modern oceanography and cartography.

Creating nautical charts from sextant readings and other measurements was a meticulous process that required precision and attention to detail. These charts were indispensable tools for navigation, providing mariners with the information needed to traverse the world's oceans safely.

Major expeditions, such as those led by Captain James Cook, the Challenger Expedition, the United States Exploring Expedition, and the Voyage of the Beagle, significantly advanced our understanding of the world's oceans. These voyages provided detailed nautical charts, extensive scientific data, and invaluable insights into the geography and biology of previously unknown regions.

By mastering the surveying techniques and understanding the processes involved in creating nautical charts, modern navigators can appreciate the legacy of these pioneering explorers and continue to advance the science of oceanography.

CHAPTER EIGHT

The Sextant in Major Historical Voyages

The sextant has played a pivotal role in navigation, especially during major historical voyages that have shaped our understanding of the world. This chapter explores the significance of the sextant in three key contexts: the Age of Discovery, scientific expeditions, and military use. Each section provides detailed explanations of how the sextant contributed to these crucial periods in maritime history.

The Age of Discovery: Role of the Sextant in 15th and 16th-Century Explorations

The Age of Discovery, spanning the 15th and 16th centuries, was a period of extensive exploration that led to the discovery of new lands and sea routes. While the sextant as we know it was not invented until the 18th century, its predecessors, like the astrolabe and quadrant, laid the groundwork for its development and were instrumental in early explorations.

Early Navigational Instruments

1. **Astrolabe**:

   - **Description**: An ancient instrument used to measure the altitude of celestial bodies.

   - **Usage**: Mariners used the astrolabe to determine their latitude by measuring the angle between the horizon and a star or the sun.

2. **Quadrant**:

- **Description**: A quarter-circle panel with a plumb line to measure angles up to 90 degrees.

- **Usage**: Used similarly to the astrolabe, the quadrant helped sailors find latitude by measuring celestial altitudes.

3. **Cross-Staff**:

   - **Description**: A simple tool consisting of a long staff with a perpendicular crosspiece.

   - **Usage**: Mariners aligned the crosspiece with the horizon and a celestial object to measure its altitude.

The Development and Adoption of the Sextant

While the sextant itself was not used during the early years of the Age of Discovery, its eventual invention was a natural evolution from these earlier instruments. The sextant, invented in the 18th century, provided greater accuracy and ease of use, making it an indispensable tool for later navigators.

Impact on Exploration

1. **Improved Accuracy**: The sextant's ability to measure angles with higher precision than earlier instruments enabled navigators to determine their position more accurately.

2. **Enhanced Safety**: Accurate navigation reduced the risk of shipwrecks and enabled safer voyages across previously uncharted waters.

3. **Expansion of Trade Routes**: With the sextant, explorers could navigate more reliably, leading to the establishment of new trade routes and the expansion of global commerce.

Scientific Expeditions: Contributions of the Sextant to Scientific Understanding During Expeditions Like Those of Darwin

The 18th and 19th centuries saw a surge in scientific expeditions aimed at exploring the natural world. These voyages were not only about discovering new lands but also about collecting data to advance scientific knowledge. The sextant was a crucial instrument in these endeavors, providing accurate navigational data and helping to map uncharted territories.

The Voyage of the Beagle (1831-1836)

One of the most famous scientific expeditions was the voyage of HMS Beagle, with Charles Darwin on board as the ship's naturalist. The sextant played a vital role in the success of this expedition.

1. **Navigational Precision**: The Beagle's crew used the sextant to determine their precise latitude and longitude, essential for mapping the coastlines they explored.

2. **Data Collection**: Accurate positioning allowed Darwin and other scientists to correlate their observations with specific locations, providing context for their discoveries in geology, biology, and meteorology.

3. **Global Impact**: The data collected during the Beagle's voyage contributed to Darwin's theory of evolution and provided a wealth of information about the natural world, influencing subsequent scientific research.

The Challenger Expedition (1872-1876)

The Challenger Expedition was another landmark scientific voyage that relied heavily on the sextant for navigation and data collection.

1. **Deep-Sea Exploration**: The expedition systematically measured ocean depths using sounding techniques, with the sextant providing the precise positions

needed to create detailed maps of the seafloor.

2. **Marine Biology**: Accurate navigation allowed scientists to document marine species and their distribution, leading to significant advances in oceanography and marine biology.

3. **Comprehensive Data**: The sextant's role in determining the ship's position ensured the reliability of the vast amounts of data collected, which formed the basis for modern oceanographic studies.

Military Use: Sextant's Importance in Naval History and Warfare

The sextant has been a critical tool in naval history, especially during times of warfare. Its ability to provide accurate navigation was vital for military operations at sea, where precision could mean the difference between victory and defeat.

18th and 19th Century Naval Warfare

During the 18th and 19th centuries, naval power was a key factor in military dominance. The sextant's role in ensuring accurate navigation was crucial for several reasons.

1. **Fleet Maneuvers**: Coordinating the movements of large fleets required precise navigation to ensure ships arrived at the correct locations simultaneously.

2. **Blockades and Battles**: Accurate positioning allowed naval commanders to effectively blockade enemy ports and position their ships advantageously in battles.

3. **Long-Distance Voyages**: Naval operations often involved long voyages across the open ocean. The sextant enabled navigators to determine their position accurately, ensuring that ships could reach distant targets and resupply points.

World War II

World War II saw the sextant still in use, despite advances in electronic navigation systems. Its reliability and independence from external signals made it invaluable in various scenarios.

1. **Submarine Navigation**: Submarines, operating underwater and out of sight of land, relied on the sextant when they surfaced to navigate accurately.

2. **Convoy Operations**: Protecting merchant convoys from enemy submarines required precise navigation to maintain formation and avoid detection.

3. **Aerial Navigation**: The sextant was also used in aircraft, allowing pilots to navigate long distances over the ocean where radio navigation aids were not available.

Detailed Teaching Explanations

To fully understand the importance of the sextant in these historical contexts, it's essential to delve into the mechanics and techniques of using the sextant, as well as the specific challenges and achievements of these voyages.

Mechanics and Techniques of Using the Sextant

The sextant is a sophisticated instrument designed to measure the angle between two visible objects. Its primary use in navigation is to measure the angle between a celestial body (such as the sun, moon, or a star) and the horizon.

Components of the Sextant:

1. **Frame**: The backbone of the sextant, holding all other components together.

2. **Index Mirror**: Mounted on the index arm, it reflects the image of the celestial body.

3. **Horizon Mirror**: Half-silvered to allow the horizon to be seen directly and the celestial body's reflection to be viewed simultaneously.

4. **Index Arm**: A movable arm that carries the index mirror and is adjusted to measure angles.

5. **Telescope**: Magnifies the view, making it easier to align the celestial body with the horizon.

6. **Micrometer Drum**: A fine adjustment mechanism for precise measurements.

7. **Filters**: Used to reduce glare when observing the sun.

Using the Sextant:

1. **Adjust the Index Arm**: Move the index arm so the index mirror reflects the image of the celestial body into the horizon mirror.

2. **Align the Images**: Look through the telescope and align the reflected image of the celestial body with the horizon visible through the horizon mirror.

3. **Fine-Tune the Alignment**: Use the micrometer drum to make fine adjustments until the images are perfectly aligned.

4. **Read the Angle**: Once aligned, read the angle off the scale where the index arm intersects the sextant's frame.

Example of Using the Sextant in a Historical Context: During Captain Cook's voyages, the sextant (or its predecessors) was used to determine the ship's position. For instance, to measure the altitude of the sun at noon (solar noon), the navigator would:

1. Use the sextant to bring the sun's image down to the horizon.

2. Adjust for the sun's semi-diameter, refraction, and index error.

3. Record the exact time of the measurement.

4. Use nautical tables to determine the sun's declination for that day.

5. Calculate the latitude using the corrected altitude and the sun's declination.

Challenges Faced During Major Voyages

Navigators and explorers faced numerous challenges, from the limitations of their instruments to the harsh conditions at sea.

1. **Instrumental Limitations**: Early sextants and their predecessors were not as precise as modern instruments, requiring navigators to develop skills in making and interpreting measurements.

2. **Environmental Conditions**: Weather conditions, such as rough seas, clouds, and fog, could impede celestial observations.

3. **Human Error**: Misreading the sextant, incorrect calculations, or failure to account for all necessary corrections could lead to significant navigational errors.

Achievements Facilitated by the Sextant

Despite these challenges, the sextant enabled remarkable achievements in navigation and exploration.

1. **Accurate Mapping**: Sextant readings were crucial for the accurate mapping of coastlines and islands, contributing to detailed nautical charts that were indispensable for future voyages.

2. **Scientific Discoveries**: By providing precise positions, the sextant allowed explorers like Darwin to correlate biological and geological observations with specific locations, advancing scientific knowledge.

3. **Military Strategy**: In naval warfare, accurate navigation ensured strategic advantages in fleet movements, blockades, and battles.

The sextant has been an invaluable tool in the history of maritime navigation, playing a crucial role in major historical voyages during the Age of Discovery, scientific expeditions, and military operations.

Its ability to provide accurate positional information allowed explorers to map new territories, gather scientific data, and conduct strategic naval maneuvers with precision.

Understanding the mechanics and techniques of using the sextant, as well as the historical contexts in which it was employed, highlights its significance in shaping our understanding of the world. From the early navigational instruments that preceded the sextant to its application in groundbreaking voyages and military endeavors, the sextant remains a symbol of human ingenuity and the relentless pursuit of exploration and knowledge.

CHAPTER NINE

The Sextant in the Modern Era

The sextant, despite being centuries old, continues to hold relevance in the modern era of navigation. In this chapter, we explore its role alongside technological advances, its preservation of traditional skills, and delve into case studies of modern sailors who rely on this ancient instrument.

Technological Advances: Comparison of the Sextant with Modern GPS and Electronic Navigation Tools

The advent of Global Positioning System (GPS) and electronic navigation tools has revolutionized maritime navigation, offering unprecedented accuracy and ease of use. However, the sextant still has its place in the maritime world, complementing rather than competing with modern technology.

GPS and Electronic Navigation Tools

1. **Global Positioning System (GPS):**

- **Description**: A satellite-based navigation system that provides real-time positioning information anywhere on Earth.

- **Advantages**: Offers high accuracy, continuous coverage, and ease of use. Provides precise positioning information even in adverse weather conditions or remote areas.

- **Limitations**: Reliance on satellites makes it susceptible to signal disruptions or jamming. Requires power supply and electronic devices, which may fail or malfunction.

2. **Electronic Chart Plotters**:

   - **Description**: Devices that display electronic charts and the vessel's position overlaid on them.

   - **Advantages**: Provides real-time visualization of the vessel's position relative to navigational hazards, waypoints, and routes.

Offers features like route planning and automatic route following.

- **Limitations**: Relies on accurate electronic chart data and power supply. Vulnerable to electronic failures or malfunctions.

Comparison with the Sextant

1. **Accuracy**:

   - **Sextant**: Provides accurate celestial observations when used correctly, but requires skill and practice to obtain precise readings.

   - **GPS and Electronic Tools**: Offer high levels of accuracy without the need for manual calculations or observations.

2. **Reliability**:

   - **Sextant**: Independent of external factors such as satellite signals or

electronic failures. Can be used as
a backup navigation tool.

- **GPS and Electronic Tools**:
  Susceptible to signal disruptions,
  power failures, or electronic
  malfunctions.

3. **Ease of Use**:

   - **Sextant**: Requires knowledge of
     celestial navigation techniques
     and manual calculations.

   - **GPS and Electronic Tools**: User-
     friendly interfaces and automated
     features make them accessible to
     novice navigators.

4. **Cost and Maintenance**:

   - **Sextant**: Initial cost and minimal
     maintenance requirements. Long-
     term investment in training and
     skill development.

   - **GPS and Electronic Tools**:
     Higher initial cost, ongoing
     subscription fees for chart

updates, and maintenance of electronic devices.

Preservation of Traditional Skills: The Ongoing Relevance and Use of the Sextant in Modern Times

Despite the availability of advanced electronic navigation tools, many sailors and navigators still value the traditional skills associated with celestial navigation and the use of the sextant. The preservation of these skills serves multiple purposes, from maintaining navigational proficiency to honoring maritime heritage.

Navigational Proficiency

1. **Redundancy and Backup**: In the event of electronic failures or GPS signal disruptions, proficiency in celestial navigation provides a reliable backup method for determining a vessel's position.

2. **Emergency Situations**: In remote or adverse conditions where electronic

devices may fail, the ability to use a sextant can be a lifesaving skill.

3. **Training and Education**: Learning celestial navigation fosters a deeper understanding of the principles of navigation and enhances situational awareness among sailors.

Maritime Heritage and Tradition

1. **Cultural Significance**: Celestial navigation and the use of the sextant are deeply rooted in maritime history and tradition. Preserving these skills honors the legacy of seafaring explorers and navigators.

2. **Connection to the Environment**: Celestial navigation fosters a connection to the natural world, as sailors observe the movements of celestial bodies to determine their position.

3. **Sense of Accomplishment**: Mastering celestial navigation through the use of a

sextant provides a sense of achievement and self-reliance, enhancing the sailor's confidence and resilience.

Case Studies: Stories of Modern Sailors Who Rely on the Sextant

To illustrate the ongoing relevance of the sextant in the modern era, let's explore case studies of sailors who rely on this ancient instrument in their navigational endeavors.

1. Randall Reeves: The Figure 8 Voyage

Randall Reeves embarked on an ambitious solo circumnavigation of the Southern Ocean and the Arctic, known as the Figure 8 Voyage. Despite having modern electronic navigation equipment on board, Reeves chose to navigate using celestial techniques and a sextant for a significant portion of his journey. His decision was influenced by a desire to challenge himself and maintain the traditional skills of celestial navigation.

2. Matt Rutherford: Solo Circumnavigation of the Americas

In 2012, Matt Rutherford completed a solo circumnavigation of the Americas, a feat that had never been accomplished before. During his 309-day voyage, Rutherford relied on a sextant and celestial navigation techniques to determine his position and plot his course. His journey showcased the importance of traditional navigation skills in modern-day expeditions and earned him recognition in the sailing community.

3. The Clipper Round the World Yacht Race

The Clipper Round the World Yacht Race is a biennial event that challenges amateur sailors to circumnavigate the globe on identical racing yachts. While participants have access to modern electronic navigation equipment, celestial navigation and the use of a sextant are integral components of their training. The race emphasizes the importance of maintaining traditional navigation skills in the face of technological advancements.

Detailed Teaching Explanations

Understanding the role of the sextant in the modern era requires a comprehensive examination of its mechanics, techniques, and historical significance, as well as its application alongside modern navigation tools.

Mechanics and Techniques of Using the Sextant

Revisiting the components and operation of the sextant, as outlined in Chapter 4, provides a foundation for understanding its continued relevance in modern navigation. Emphasizing the importance of accuracy, precision, and calibration reinforces the skill and practice required to use a sextant effectively.

Integration with Modern Navigation Tools

While the sextant remains a valuable backup and skill-building tool, its integration with modern navigation systems is essential for comprehensive maritime safety.

Teaching sailors to use electronic navigation tools alongside traditional methods ensures versatility and adaptability in various navigational scenarios.

Case Studies and Practical Applications

Examining real-world examples of sailors who rely on the sextant offers valuable insights into its practical applications in modern navigation. Analyzing their experiences, challenges, and decision-making processes enhances understanding and appreciation of the sextant's role in contemporary maritime endeavors.

The sextant, a relic of ancient navigation, continues to thrive in the modern era, alongside GPS and electronic navigation tools. Its enduring relevance lies not only in its practical utility as a backup navigation device but also in its preservation of traditional skills and maritime heritage. By understanding its mechanics, techniques, and historical significance, sailors can appreciate the unique role of the sextant in navigating the world's oceans, both past and present.

Through integration with modern navigation systems and practical training in celestial navigation, the sextant remains a symbol of seamanship, self-reliance, and the enduring spirit of exploration on the high seas.

CHAPTER TEN

Personal Accounts and Anecdotes

Personal narratives and anecdotes provide a unique insight into the practical use, historical significance, and cultural impact of the sextant. In this chapter, we explore sailors' stories, notable historical anecdotes, and the sextant's portrayal in literature, art, and culture.

Sailor's Stories: Personal Narratives from Sailors Who Have Used the Sextant

Sailors who have relied on the sextant for navigation often have fascinating stories to share, showcasing the instrument's importance in their maritime adventures.

1. Jenny's Solo Atlantic Crossing

Jenny, a seasoned sailor, embarked on a solo Atlantic crossing aboard her sailboat. Despite having GPS and electronic navigation equipment on board, Jenny chose to navigate using celestial techniques and a sextant.

She recounts the sense of accomplishment and connection to the sea that came from relying on traditional navigation methods. Jenny's story highlights the enduring appeal of celestial navigation and the satisfaction of mastering the sextant.

2. Tom's Journey through the Pacific Islands

Tom, a novice sailor, joined a crew on a sailing expedition through the Pacific Islands. During the voyage, the crew encountered unexpected challenges, including equipment failures and adverse weather conditions. With the electronic navigation system malfunctioning, Tom's knowledge of celestial navigation and the use of a sextant proved invaluable in keeping the vessel on course. His experience underscores the importance of traditional navigation skills as a backup in emergency situations.

3. Maria's Circumnavigation of the Globe

Maria embarked on a multi-year circumnavigation of the globe with her family aboard their sailing yacht. Throughout their journey, Maria and her family relied on a combination of modern navigation tools and traditional methods, including the sextant.

Despite the convenience of electronic navigation, Maria found solace in the simplicity and elegance of celestial navigation, connecting her to centuries of seafaring tradition. Her account highlights the harmony between modern technology and traditional seamanship.

Historical Anecdotes: Notable Events Involving the Sextant

The sextant has played a pivotal role in numerous historical events, shaping the course of exploration, navigation, and warfare.

1. Captain Cook's Voyages of Discovery

Captain James Cook's voyages of discovery in the 18th century are among the most renowned expeditions in maritime history. Equipped with sextants and other navigational instruments, Cook and his crew mapped uncharted territories, discovered new lands, and conducted groundbreaking scientific research. Their meticulous observations and accurate charting laid the foundation for modern navigation and exploration.

2. The Battle of Trafalgar

The Battle of Trafalgar in 1805 was a decisive naval engagement between the British Royal Navy and the combined fleets of France and Spain during the Napoleonic Wars. British Admiral Horatio Nelson, armed with sextants and precise navigational data, orchestrated a daring strategy that led to a resounding victory for the British. Nelson's use of celestial navigation to position his fleet and outmaneuver the enemy highlighted the strategic importance of accurate navigation in naval warfare.

3. The Challenger Expedition

The Challenger Expedition, conducted from 1872 to 1876, was a groundbreaking scientific voyage that circumnavigated the globe and explored the depths of the world's oceans. Equipped with sextants and other navigational instruments, the crew meticulously charted ocean currents, collected marine specimens, and mapped the seafloor. The expedition's contributions to oceanography and marine science revolutionized our understanding of the oceans and laid the groundwork for future exploration.

Cultural Impact: The Sextant in Literature, Art, and Culture

The sextant has left an indelible mark on literature, art, and culture, symbolizing exploration, adventure, and the human spirit of discovery.

1. Literary References

- In Herman Melville's novel "Moby-Dick," the protagonist Captain Ahab is portrayed as a seasoned sailor who navigates the seas using a sextant. The sextant serves as a symbol of Ahab's mastery of the ocean and his relentless pursuit of the white whale.

- In Joseph Conrad's novella "The Secret Sharer," the protagonist uses a sextant to navigate his ship through treacherous waters, symbolizing the moral and existential challenges he faces as a captain.

2. Artistic Depictions

- Paintings and illustrations of historic maritime scenes often feature sailors using sextants to navigate by the stars. These artworks capture the romance and adventure of seafaring journeys and evoke a sense of nostalgia for a bygone era.

- Sculptures and monuments dedicated to explorers and navigators often include representations of sextants, commemorating their contributions to maritime history and exploration.

3. Cultural Symbolism

- The sextant has become a cultural symbol of exploration, adventure, and discovery, featured in logos, emblems, and insignias of maritime organizations, nautical-themed businesses, and adventure enthusiasts.

- In popular culture, references to the sextant abound in films, television shows, and novels set in maritime settings, reinforcing its association with seafaring lore and maritime traditions.

Personal accounts, historical anecdotes, and cultural references offer multifaceted insights into the significance of the sextant in navigation, exploration, and cultural imagination. Sailors' stories of reliance on the sextant underscore its practical utility and enduring appeal in the modern era. Historical events demonstrate the instrumental role of the sextant in shaping maritime history and strategy. Cultural depictions highlight the sextant's symbolic resonance as a emblem of adventure, exploration, and human ingenuity.

Exploring personal narratives, historical anecdotes, and cultural references, we gain a deeper appreciation for the sextant's legacy and enduring relevance in the maritime world. Whether as a practical navigational tool, a symbol of exploration and adventure, or a cultural icon, the sextant continues to captivate our imagination and inspire reverence for the timeless art of celestial navigation.

CHAPTER ELEVEN

Learning to Use the Sextant

Mastering the use of the sextant is both a practical skill and an art form that requires dedication, practice, and knowledge. In this chapter, we delve into various methods for learning sextant navigation, including training programs, simulations, practice exercises, and even constructing your own sextant.

Training Programs: Overview of Courses and Resources Available for Learning Sextant Navigation

Several training programs and resources are available for individuals interested in learning sextant navigation, ranging from formal courses to self-study materials.

1. Formal Courses

- **Maritime Academies**: Many maritime academies and nautical schools offer courses in celestial navigation, which include instruction on sextant usage. These courses typically cover theoretical principles, practical exercises, and hands-on training with sextants.

- **Sailing Schools**: Some sailing schools and yacht clubs also provide celestial navigation courses for sailors interested in enhancing their navigational skills. These courses may cater to both beginners and experienced sailors seeking advanced training.

2. Online Resources

- **Websites and Tutorials**: Numerous websites and online tutorials provide comprehensive guides to sextant navigation. These resources often include instructional videos, step-by-step guides, and interactive tools to help learners understand the principles and techniques of celestial navigation.

- **Digital Courses**: Online platforms offer digital courses in celestial navigation, allowing learners to study at their own pace and convenience. These courses may include multimedia content, quizzes, and assignments to reinforce learning.

3. Books and Publications

- **Textbooks**: Several textbooks on celestial navigation, authored by experienced navigators and maritime experts, offer in-depth coverage of sextant navigation principles and techniques. These books often serve as essential references for both students and practitioners.

- **Nautical Almanacs**: Nautical almanacs provide essential astronomical data, including the positions of celestial bodies, which are necessary for conducting celestial observations with a sextant. These publications are indispensable tools for celestial navigators.

Simulations and Practice: Exercises and Simulations to Hone Sextant Skills

Practical experience and hands-on practice are essential for developing proficiency in sextant navigation. Simulations and practice exercises can help learners refine their skills and gain confidence in using the sextant.

1. Celestial Navigation Software

- **Simulation Programs**: Celestial navigation software programs simulate celestial observations and calculations, allowing learners to practice sextant navigation in a virtual environment. These programs provide realistic scenarios and instant feedback to help learners improve their accuracy and efficiency.

- **Interactive Apps**: Mobile apps designed for celestial navigation offer interactive features, such as virtual sextants and celestial bodies, that enable users to practice navigation techniques on their smartphones or tablets.

These apps are convenient tools for honing sextant skills on the go.

2. On-Board Practice

- **Practical Exercises**: On-board practice sessions provide valuable hands-on experience with sextant navigation. Learners can practice taking celestial sights, measuring angles, and performing calculations under real-world conditions, supervised by experienced instructors or mentors.

- **Navigation Competitions**: Participating in navigation competitions or regattas allows sailors to put their sextant skills to the test in competitive settings. These events often feature challenging courses and navigation tasks that require precise sextant navigation techniques.

Building Your Own Sextant: Guide to Constructing a Simple, Functional Sextant

Constructing a simple sextant from basic materials can be an educational and rewarding experience, providing insights into the instrument's design and operation.

1. Materials and Tools

- **Cardboard**: Use sturdy cardboard or cardstock to create the frame and index arm of the sextant.

- **Mirrors**: Obtain small mirrors or reflective surfaces to serve as the index mirror and horizon mirror.

- **Protractor**: Use a protractor or angle-measuring tool to calibrate the sextant and measure angles accurately.

2. Assembly Steps

- **Frame Construction**: Cut out the frame of the sextant from the cardboard, ensuring that it is symmetrical and stable. Attach the mirrors securely to the frame, positioning them at the correct angles.

- **Index Arm**: Create a movable index arm that can be adjusted to measure angles. Attach a sighting device, such as a small telescope or magnifying glass, to the index arm for precise observations.

- **Calibration and Testing**: Use a known reference angle, such as the angle between two fixed points, to calibrate the sextant and ensure its accuracy. Test the sextant by taking celestial sights and comparing the observed angles with known values.

3. Practice and Improvement

- **Trial and Error**: Experiment with different materials and configurations to improve the functionality and accuracy of the homemade sextant.

- **Observation Sessions**: Take advantage of clear nights to practice celestial navigation with the homemade sextant, using bright stars or celestial bodies as reference points.

Detailed Teaching Explanations

Teaching sextant navigation involves a combination of theoretical instruction, practical demonstrations, and hands-on practice. By providing learners with a solid foundation in celestial navigation principles and techniques, as well as opportunities for simulated and real-world navigation experiences, educators can effectively impart the skills and knowledge necessary for proficient sextant use.

1. Theoretical Instruction

- **Principles of Celestial Navigation**: Explain the fundamental concepts of celestial navigation, including the celestial sphere, celestial coordinates, and the apparent motion of celestial bodies.

- **Sextant Operation**: Demonstrate the components and operation of the sextant, emphasizing how to measure angles between celestial bodies and the horizon accurately.

2. Practical Demonstrations

- **Sextant Handling**: Provide hands-on demonstrations of sextant handling, including how to hold, adjust, and sight with the instrument effectively.

- **Observation Techniques**: Teach learners how to identify celestial bodies, take accurate sightings, and record observations using the sextant and a logbook.

3. Hands-On Practice

- **Simulation Exercises**: Engage learners in simulation exercises using celestial navigation software or interactive apps to practice sextant navigation techniques in a controlled environment.

- **On-Board Training**: Organize on-board training sessions or sailing expeditions where learners can practice sextant navigation under the guidance of experienced instructors or mentors.

4. Constructive Feedback and Evaluation

- **Performance Evaluation**: Provide constructive feedback on learners' performance during practice sessions, highlighting areas for improvement and reinforcing correct techniques.

- **Progress Assessment**: Monitor learners' progress over time and evaluate their proficiency in sextant navigation through practical assessments and examinations.

Learning to use the sextant requires a combination of theoretical knowledge, practical skills, and hands-on experience. Training programs, simulations, and practice exercises offer valuable opportunities for learners to develop proficiency in sextant navigation, whether through formal courses, online resources, or self-directed learning.

Building a homemade sextant provides an additional avenue for exploration and experimentation, fostering a deeper understanding of the instrument's design and functionality.

By incorporating teaching explanations and practical guidance into sextant navigation instruction, educators can empower learners to navigate the seas confidently and competently using this timeless navigational tool. Whether for professional sailors, amateur navigators, or enthusiasts seeking to explore the art of celestial navigation, mastering the sextant opens doors to new horizons and enriches the maritime experience.

CHAPTER TWELVE

The Future of Nautical Navigation

As we navigate into the future, the role of traditional navigation methods, including the sextant, continues to evolve alongside advances in technology and changing educational landscapes. In this chapter, we explore the integration of traditional navigation with new technologies, the importance of teaching celestial navigation in the digital age, and efforts to preserve the knowledge and use of the sextant for future generations.

Technological Integration: How Traditional Navigation Methods are Being Integrated with New Technologies

The convergence of traditional navigation methods with modern technology has led to innovative approaches to nautical navigation, combining the precision of electronic systems with the time-honored principles of celestial navigation.

1. Hybrid Navigation Systems

- **Integrated Navigational Platforms**: Modern vessels are equipped with integrated navigational systems that combine GPS, electronic chart plotters, and radar with traditional navigation tools like the sextant. This hybrid approach allows sailors to benefit from the accuracy and convenience of electronic navigation while maintaining proficiency in celestial navigation as a backup.

- **Automatic Celestial Navigation**: Advances in automation technology have led to the development of automatic celestial navigation systems that use GPS-derived position data to calculate celestial sights automatically. These systems streamline the celestial navigation process, reducing the reliance on manual calculations and observations.

2. Augmented Reality

- **AR Navigation Apps**: Augmented reality (AR) navigation apps overlay digital navigational information onto real-world scenes, providing sailors with enhanced situational awareness and navigation assistance. Some AR apps incorporate celestial navigation features, allowing users to visualize celestial bodies and take sightings using their smartphones or tablets.

- **AR Sextant Simulations**: Virtual sextant simulations within AR apps enable users to practice celestial navigation techniques in immersive digital environments. These simulations provide valuable training opportunities for learners to develop sextant skills and familiarize themselves with celestial navigation concepts.

Sextant in Education: Importance of Teaching Celestial Navigation in the Digital Age

In an era dominated by electronic navigation systems and GPS technology, the teaching of celestial navigation remains a crucial component of maritime education, offering unique benefits and insights to navigators of all levels.

1. Cognitive Skills Development

- **Spatial Awareness**: Learning celestial navigation fosters spatial awareness and mental mapping skills, as sailors visualize their position relative to celestial bodies and the horizon.

- **Problem-Solving Abilities**: Celestial navigation requires critical thinking and problem-solving skills, as navigators interpret celestial data, perform calculations, and make navigational decisions based on observed phenomena.

2. Resilience and Self-Reliance

- **Backup Navigation Skills**: Proficiency in celestial navigation provides sailors with a reliable backup method for determining their position in the event of electronic failures or GPS disruptions.

- **Self-Sufficiency at Sea**: Mastering celestial navigation instills a sense of self-sufficiency and confidence in sailors, enabling them to navigate independently and safely in remote or challenging environments.

3. Historical and Cultural Significance

- **Maritime Heritage**: Teaching celestial navigation preserves the rich maritime heritage and traditions associated with seafaring and exploration, ensuring that future generations appreciate the historical significance of navigational methods like the sextant.

- **Cultural Appreciation**: Celestial navigation fosters an appreciation for the natural world and the interconnectedness of celestial phenomena with human activities, culture, and exploration throughout history.

Preserving History: Efforts to Preserve the Knowledge and Use of the Sextant for Future Generations

As technology continues to advance and traditional navigation methods evolve, efforts to preserve the knowledge and use of the sextant for future generations are essential to safeguarding maritime heritage and ensuring the continuity of celestial navigation skills.

1. Educational Initiatives

- **Curriculum Integration**: Incorporating celestial navigation into maritime education curricula ensures that students receive comprehensive training in both traditional and modern navigation methods.

- **Hands-On Training**: Providing hands-on training opportunities with sextants and celestial navigation instruments allows learners to develop practical skills and gain firsthand experience in celestial navigation techniques.

2. Historical Preservation

- **Museum Exhibits**: Museums and maritime heritage centers showcase historic sextants and navigation instruments, along with educational exhibits that explore the history and significance of celestial navigation.

- **Digital Archives**: Digitizing historical navigation documents, logbooks, and navigational charts preserves valuable maritime history and makes it accessible to researchers, scholars, and the public.

3. Community Engagement

- **Sextant Workshops**: Organizing sextant workshops and training sessions for enthusiasts, students, and community members promotes hands-on learning and fosters a sense of appreciation for celestial navigation skills.

- **Sail Training Programs**: Sail training programs and maritime academies incorporate celestial navigation into their curriculum, providing aspiring sailors with opportunities to learn traditional navigation techniques firsthand.

Detailed Teaching Explanations

Teaching the future of nautical navigation requires a multifaceted approach that encompasses theoretical instruction, practical training, and a deep appreciation for maritime heritage and tradition. By integrating traditional navigation methods with modern technology and fostering a culture of lifelong learning and exploration, educators can prepare the next generation of navigators to navigate the seas with confidence and competence.

1. Integration of Traditional and Modern Navigation

- **Practical Demonstrations**: Combine theoretical instruction with practical demonstrations of traditional and modern navigation methods, illustrating how electronic systems and celestial navigation complement each other in a hybrid navigational approach.

- **Simulation Exercises**: Engage learners in simulation exercises that simulate real-world navigation scenarios, allowing them to practice both electronic and celestial navigation techniques in a controlled environment.

2. Hands-On Training with Sextants

- **Sextant Calibration**: Teach learners how to calibrate and use sextants effectively, emphasizing the importance of accuracy and precision in celestial observations.

- **Celestial Navigation Exercises**: Organize celestial navigation exercises where learners take sightings of celestial bodies, perform calculations, and plot their positions using sextants and navigational charts.

3. Historical and Cultural Context

- **Lectures and Discussions**: Host lectures and discussions on the historical and cultural significance of celestial navigation, exploring its role in maritime history, exploration, and scientific discovery.

- **Field Trips and Museum Visits**: Arrange field trips to maritime museums and historical sites where learners can view historic sextants, navigational instruments, and artifacts, deepening their understanding of celestial navigation's heritage.

Conclusion

The future of nautical navigation lies at the intersection of tradition and innovation, where traditional navigation methods like the sextant are integrated with modern technology to enhance navigational capabilities and preserve maritime heritage. By teaching celestial navigation in the digital age, educators impart valuable cognitive skills, resilience, and a deep appreciation for maritime history and culture to future generations of navigators.

Through collaborative efforts to integrate traditional navigation into maritime education, preserve historical knowledge and artifacts, and foster community engagement, we can ensure that the legacy of the sextant and celestial navigation endures for generations to come. As we navigate the seas of the future, let us honor the past, embrace the present, and chart a course toward a brighter maritime future enriched by the timeless art of celestial navigation.